TULSA CITY-COUNTY LIBRARY

American Mastodon

by Julie Murray

ICE AGE ANIMALS

Abdo Kids Jumbo is an Imprint of Abdo Kids
abdobooks.com

abdobooks.com

Published by Abdo Kids, a division of ABDO, P.O. Box 398166, Minneapolis, Minnesota 55439. Copyright © 2024 by Abdo Consulting Group, Inc. International copyrights reserved in all countries. No part of this book may be reproduced in any form without written permission from the publisher. Abdo Kids Jumbo™ is a trademark and logo of Abdo Kids.

Printed in the United States of America, North Mankato, Minnesota.

052023

092023

 THIS BOOK CONTAINS RECYCLED MATERIALS

Photo Credits: Alamy, National Park Service, Science Source, Shutterstock, ©Barry Roal Carlsen p.17 ©Dantheman9758 p.cover / CC BY-SA 3.0, ©James St. John p.1 / CC BY 2.0, ©Roman Uchytel p.13

Production Contributors: Teddy Borth, Jennie Forsberg, Grace Hansen
Design Contributors: Candice Keimig, Pakou Moua

Library of Congress Control Number: 2022946807
Publisher's Cataloging-in-Publication Data

Names: Murray, Julie, author.

Title: American mastodon / by Julie Murray

Description: Minneapolis, Minnesota : Abdo Kids, 2024 | Series: Ice age animals | Includes online resources and index.

Identifiers: ISBN 9781098266325 (lib. bdg.) | ISBN 9781098267025 (ebook) | ISBN 9781098267377 (Read-to-me ebook)

Subjects: LCSH: Animals--Juvenile literature. | Extinct animals--Juvenile literature. | Ice Age--Juvenile literature. | Paleontology--Juvenile literature. | Zoology--Juvenile literature.

Classification: DDC 569--dc23

Table of Contents

Ice Age 4

American Mastodon 6

Food 16

Extinction 20

More Facts 22

Glossary 23

Index 24

Abdo Kids Code. 24

Ice Age

An ice age is a period when most of the Earth is covered in sheets of ice. The last ice age began about 100,000 years ago. It lasted until about 12,000 years ago. Some animals became **extinct** during this time in history.

American Mastodon

The American mastodon was an elephant-like animal. It lived throughout North America. It was found in forests and wetlands.

The American mastodon was big! It stood 7 to 10 feet (2.1 to 3 m) tall. It weighed 8,000 to 12,000 pounds (3,629 to 5,443 kg). Males were larger than females.

The American mastodon had a low-domed head with small ears. It had a long, flexible nose. Its thick legs and muscular body made it a **stocky** animal.

Its body was covered in thick, shaggy brown fur. The fur kept it warm in the cold temperatures.

The American mastodon had long tusks. The tusks had a slight curve. They could grow to be over 15 feet (4.8 m) long! The mastodon used its tusks to break branches.

Food

The American mastodon was a plant eater. It enjoyed eating leaves and twigs. It also ate branches and pine needles.

The mastodon had **unique** teeth. The **molars** were cone-shaped. These were perfect for eating leaves, twigs, and smaller vegetation.

Extinction

The American mastodon became **extinct** about 13,000 years ago. **Climate change** was the biggest reason for this. Humans also played a role. They hunted it for food and to make clothes, tools, and weapons.

More Facts

- The first American mastodon fossils were found in 1705. The fossils were discovered in the Hudson River Valley in New York.

- The American mastodon walked on its tiptoes like a modern elephant.

- It lived in a group that consisted of females and their young. Males left the group around age 10 to live on their own.

- Some think that human disease contributed to the animal's extinction. Many fossils found have shown the presence of tuberculosis.

Glossary

climate change – a change in global and regional climate patterns.

extinct – no longer existing.

fossil – the remains or trace of a living animal or plant from a long time ago.

molar – a large tooth located in the back of the mouth, with a broad biting surface used for grinding food.

stocky – thick, sturdy, and often short.

tuberculosis – a serious disease that is passed through the air. It usually affects the lungs.

unique – different from everything else.

Index

body 10, 12

climate change 20

color 12

ears 10

females 8

food 16, 18

fur 12

habitat 6

head 10

legs 10

males 8

nose 10

range 6

size 8

teeth 18

tusks 14

weight 8

Visit **abdokids.com** to access crafts, games, videos, and more!

Use Abdo Kids code **IAK6325** or scan this QR code!